Mileage Logbook

Name:	Position:
Adress:	
Mobile:	
Telephone:	
Email:	
Fax:	

Book info :

Book No.:	
Start Date:	End Date:

Notes:

Vehicle Mileage Logbook

Sheet no.:

Make :	Model :	Year :	License number :

DATE	PURPOSE OF TRAVEL	JOURNEY		ODOMETER READING			TOTAL MILES	
		From	To	Start	End	Distance (km)	Business	Private

Daily checks	Tires/ Wheel	Wipers	Lights	Mirrors	Horn	Seatbelts	Brakes	Coupling devices
Monday								
Tuesday								
Wednesday								
Thursday								
Friday								
Saturday								
Sunday								

Fuel Input				
Date	Quantity	Unit	Mileage	Units

Notes :

Signature :

Vehicle Mileage Logbook

Vehicle Mileage Logbook	Sheet no.:

Make :	Model :	Year :	License number :

DATE	PURPOSE OF TRAVEL	JOURNEY		ODOMETER READING			TOTAL MILES	
		From	To	Start	End	Distance (km)	Business	Private

Daily checks	Tires/ Wheel	Wipers	Lights	Mirrors	Horn	Seatbelts	Brakes	Coupling devices
Monday								
Tuesday								
Wednesday								
Thursday								
Friday								
Saturday								
Sunday								

Fuel Input				
Date	Quantity	Unit	Mileage	Units

Notes :

Signature :

Vehicle Mileage Logbook

Sheet no.:

Make :	Model :	Year :	License number :

DATE	PURPOSE OF TRAVEL	JOURNEY		ODOMETER READING			TOTAL MILES	
		From	To	Start	End	Distance (km)	Business	Private

Daily checks	Tires/ Wheel	Wipers	Lights	Mirrors	Horn	Seatbelts	Brakes	Coupling devices
Monday								
Tuesday								
Wednesday								
Thursday								
Friday								
Saturday								
Sunday								

Fuel Input				
Date	Quantity	Unit	Mileage	Units

Notes :

Signature :

Vehicle Mileage Logbook

Vehicle Mileage Logbook			Sheet no.:
Make :	Model :	Year :	License number :

DATE	PURPOSE OF TRAVEL	JOURNEY		ODOMETER READING			TOTAL MILES	
		From	To	Start	End	Distance (km)	Business	Private

Daily checks	Tires/ Wheel	Wipers	Lights	Mirrors	Horn	Seatbelts	Brakes	Coupling devices
Monday								
Tuesday								
Wednesday								
Thursday								
Friday								
Saturday								
Sunday								

Fuel Input				
Date	Quantity	Unit	Mileage	Units

Notes :

Signature :

Vehicle Mileage Logbook

Sheet no.:

Make :	Model :	Year :	License number :

DATE	PURPOSE OF TRAVEL	JOURNEY		ODOMETER READING			TOTAL MILES	
		From	To	Start	End	Distance (km)	Business	Private

Daily checks	Tires/ Wheel	Wipers	Lights	Mirrors	Horn	Seatbelts	Brakes	Coupling devices
Monday								
Tuesday								
Wednesday								
Thursday								
Friday								
Saturday								
Sunday								

Fuel Input				
Date	Quantity	Unit	Mileage	Units

Notes :

Signature :

Vehicle Mileage Logbook

Sheet no.:

Make :	Model :	Year :	License number :

DATE	PURPOSE OF TRAVEL	JOURNEY		ODOMETER READING			TOTAL MILES	
		From	To	Start	End	Distance (km)	Business	Private

Daily checks	Tires/ Wheel	Wipers	Lights	Mirrors	Horn	Seatbelts	Brakes	Coupling devices
Monday								
Tuesday								
Wednesday								
Thursday								
Friday								
Saturday								
Sunday								

Fuel Input				
Date	Quantity	Unit	Mileage	Units

Notes :

Signature :

Vehicle Mileage Logbook

Vehicle Mileage Logbook	Sheet no.:

Make :	Model :	Year :	License number :

DATE	PURPOSE OF TRAVEL	JOURNEY		ODOMETER READING			TOTAL MILES	
		From	To	Start	End	Distance (km)	Business	Private

Daily checks	Tires/ Wheel	Wipers	Lights	Mirrors	Horn	Seatbelts	Brakes	Coupling devices
Monday								
Tuesday								
Wednesday								
Thursday								
Friday								
Saturday								
Sunday								

Fuel Input				
Date	Quantity	Unit	Mileage	Units

Notes :

Signature :

Vehicle Mileage Logbook

Sheet no.:

Make : | Model : | Year : | License number :

DATE	PURPOSE OF TRAVEL	JOURNEY		ODOMETER READING			TOTAL MILES	
		From	To	Start	End	Distance (km)	Business	Private

Daily checks	Tires/ Wheel	Wipers	Lights	Mirrors	Horn	Seatbelts	Brakes	Coupling devices
Monday								
Tuesday								
Wednesday								
Thursday								
Friday								
Saturday								
Sunday								

Fuel Input				
Date	Quantity	Unit	Mileage	Units

Notes :

Signature :

Vehicle Mileage Logbook

Sheet no.:

Make :	Model :	Year :	License number :

DATE	PURPOSE OF TRAVEL	JOURNEY		ODOMETER READING			TOTAL MILES	
		From	To	Start	End	Distance (km)	Business	Private

Daily checks	Tires/ Wheel	Wipers	Lights	Mirrors	Horn	Seatbelts	Brakes	Coupling devices
Monday								
Tuesday								
Wednesday								
Thursday								
Friday								
Saturday								
Sunday								

Fuel Input				
Date	Quantity	Unit	Mileage	Units

Notes :

Signature :

Vehicle Mileage Logbook

Sheet no.:

Make :	Model :	Year :	License number :

DATE	PURPOSE OF TRAVEL	JOURNEY		ODOMETER READING			TOTAL MILES	
		From	To	Start	End	Distance (km)	Business	Private

Daily checks	Tires/ Wheel	Wipers	Lights	Mirrors	Horn	Seatbelts	Brakes	Coupling devices
Monday								
Tuesday								
Wednesday								
Thursday								
Friday								
Saturday								
Sunday								

Fuel Input				
Date	Quantity	Unit	Mileage	Units

Notes :

Signature :

Vehicle Mileage Logbook

Sheet no.:

Make :	Model :	Year :	License number :

DATE	PURPOSE OF TRAVEL	JOURNEY		ODOMETER READING			TOTAL MILES	
		From	To	Start	End	Distance (km)	Business	Private

Daily checks	Tires/ Wheel	Wipers	Lights	Mirrors	Horn	Seatbelts	Brakes	Coupling devices
Monday								
Tuesday								
Wednesday								
Thursday								
Friday								
Saturday								
Sunday								

Fuel Input				
Date	Quantity	Unit	Mileage	Units

Notes :

Signature :

Vehicle Mileage Logbook

Sheet no.:

Make : | Model : | Year : | License number :

DATE	PURPOSE OF TRAVEL	JOURNEY		ODOMETER READING			TOTAL MILES	
		From	To	Start	End	Distance (km)	Business	Private

Daily checks	Tires/ Wheel	Wipers	Lights	Mirrors	Horn	Seatbelts	Brakes	Coupling devices
Monday								
Tuesday								
Wednesday								
Thursday								
Friday								
Saturday								
Sunday								

Fuel Input				
Date	Quantity	Unit	Mileage	Units

Notes :

Signature :

Vehicle Mileage Logbook

Sheet no.:

Make :	Model :	Year :	License number :

DATE	PURPOSE OF TRAVEL	JOURNEY		ODOMETER READING			TOTAL MILES	
		From	To	Start	End	Distance (km)	Business	Private

Daily checks	Tires/ Wheel	Wipers	Lights	Mirrors	Horn	Seatbelts	Brakes	Coupling devices
Monday								
Tuesday								
Wednesday								
Thursday								
Friday								
Saturday								
Sunday								

Fuel Input				
Date	Quantity	Unit	Mileage	Units

Notes :

Signature :

Vehicle Mileage Logbook

Vehicle Mileage Logbook	Sheet no.:

Make :	Model :	Year :	License number :

DATE	PURPOSE OF TRAVEL	JOURNEY		ODOMETER READING			TOTAL MILES	
		From	To	Start	End	Distance (km)	Business	Private

Daily checks	Tires/ Wheel	Wipers	Lights	Mirrors	Horn	Seatbelts	Brakes	Coupling devices
Monday								
Tuesday								
Wednesday								
Thursday								
Friday								
Saturday								
Sunday								

Fuel Input				
Date	Quantity	Unit	Mileage	Units

Notes :

Signature :

Vehicle Mileage Logbook

Sheet no.:

Make :	Model :	Year :	License number :

DATE	PURPOSE OF TRAVEL	JOURNEY		ODOMETER READING			TOTAL MILES	
		From	To	Start	End	Distance (km)	Business	Private

Daily checks	Tires/ Wheel	Wipers	Lights	Mirrors	Horn	Seatbelts	Brakes	Coupling devices
Monday								
Tuesday								
Wednesday								
Thursday								
Friday								
Saturday								
Sunday								

Fuel Input				
Date	Quantity	Unit	Mileage	Units

Notes :

Signature :

Vehicle Mileage Logbook

Sheet no.:

Make :	Model :	Year :	License number :

DATE	PURPOSE OF TRAVEL	JOURNEY		ODOMETER READING			TOTAL MILES	
		From	To	Start	End	Distance (km)	Business	Private

Daily checks	Tires/ Wheel	Wipers	Lights	Mirrors	Horn	Seatbelts	Brakes	Coupling devices
Monday								
Tuesday								
Wednesday								
Thursday								
Friday								
Saturday								
Sunday								

Fuel Input				
Date	Quantity	Unit	Mileage	Units

Notes :

Signature :

Vehicle Mileage Logbook

Sheet no.:

Make :	Model :	Year :	License number :

DATE	PURPOSE OF TRAVEL	JOURNEY		ODOMETER READING			TOTAL MILES	
		From	To	Start	End	Distance (km)	Business	Private

Daily checks	Tires/ Wheel	Wipers	Lights	Mirrors	Horn	Seatbelts	Brakes	Coupling devices
Monday								
Tuesday								
Wednesday								
Thursday								
Friday								
Saturday								
Sunday								

Fuel Input				
Date	Quantity	Unit	Mileage	Units

Notes :

Signature :

Vehicle Mileage Logbook

Sheet no.:

Make :	Model :	Year :	License number :

DATE	PURPOSE OF TRAVEL	JOURNEY		ODOMETER READING			TOTAL MILES	
		From	To	Start	End	Distance (km)	Business	Private

Daily checks	Tires/ Wheel	Wipers	Lights	Mirrors	Horn	Seatbelts	Brakes	Coupling devices
Monday								
Tuesday								
Wednesday								
Thursday								
Friday								
Saturday								
Sunday								

Fuel Input				
Date	Quantity	Unit	Mileage	Units

Notes :

Signature :

Vehicle Mileage Logbook

Sheet no.:

Make :	Model :	Year :	License number :

DATE	PURPOSE OF TRAVEL	JOURNEY		ODOMETER READING			TOTAL MILES	
		From	To	Start	End	Distance (km)	Business	Private

Daily checks	Tires/ Wheel	Wipers	Lights	Mirrors	Horn	Seatbelts	Brakes	Coupling devices
Monday								
Tuesday								
Wednesday								
Thursday								
Friday								
Saturday								
Sunday								

Fuel Input				
Date	Quantity	Unit	Mileage	Units

Notes :

Signature :

Vehicle Mileage Logbook

Sheet no.:

Make :	Model :	Year :	License number :

DATE	PURPOSE OF TRAVEL	JOURNEY		ODOMETER READING			TOTAL MILES	
		From	To	Start	End	Distance (km)	Business	Private

Daily checks	Tires/ Wheel	Wipers	Lights	Mirrors	Horn	Seatbelts	Brakes	Coupling devices
Monday								
Tuesday								
Wednesday								
Thursday								
Friday								
Saturday								
Sunday								

Fuel Input				
Date	Quantity	Unit	Mileage	Units

Notes :

Signature :

Vehicle Mileage Logbook

Sheet no.:

Make :	Model :	Year :	License number :

DATE	PURPOSE OF TRAVEL	JOURNEY		ODOMETER READING			TOTAL MILES	
		From	To	Start	End	Distance (km)	Business	Private

Daily checks	Tires/ Wheel	Wipers	Lights	Mirrors	Horn	Seatbelts	Brakes	Coupling devices
Monday								
Tuesday								
Wednesday								
Thursday								
Friday								
Saturday								
Sunday								

Fuel Input				
Date	Quantity	Unit	Mileage	Units

Notes :

Signature :

Vehicle Mileage Logbook

Sheet no.:

Make :	Model :	Year :	License number :

DATE	PURPOSE OF TRAVEL	JOURNEY		ODOMETER READING			TOTAL MILES	
		From	To	Start	End	Distance (km)	Business	Private

Daily checks	Tires/ Wheel	Wipers	Lights	Mirrors	Horn	Seatbelts	Brakes	Coupling devices
Monday								
Tuesday								
Wednesday								
Thursday								
Friday								
Saturday								
Sunday								

Fuel Input				
Date	Quantity	Unit	Mileage	Units

Notes :

Signature :

Vehicle Mileage Logbook

Sheet no.:

Make :	Model :	Year :	License number :

DATE	PURPOSE OF TRAVEL	JOURNEY		ODOMETER READING			TOTAL MILES	
		From	To	Start	End	Distance (km)	Business	Private

Daily checks	Tires/ Wheel	Wipers	Lights	Mirrors	Horn	Seatbelts	Brakes	Coupling devices
Monday								
Tuesday								
Wednesday								
Thursday								
Friday								
Saturday								
Sunday								

Fuel Input				
Date	Quantity	Unit	Mileage	Units

Notes :

Signature :

Vehicle Mileage Logbook

Sheet no.:

Make :	Model :	Year :	License number :

DATE	PURPOSE OF TRAVEL	JOURNEY		ODOMETER READING			TOTAL MILES	
		From	To	Start	End	Distance (km)	Business	Private

Daily checks	Tires/ Wheel	Wipers	Lights	Mirrors	Horn	Seatbelts	Brakes	Coupling devices
Monday								
Tuesday								
Wednesday								
Thursday								
Friday								
Saturday								
Sunday								

Fuel Input				
Date	Quantity	Unit	Mileage	Units

Notes :

Signature :

Vehicle Mileage Logbook

Sheet no.:

Make :	Model :	Year :	License number :

DATE	PURPOSE OF TRAVEL	JOURNEY		ODOMETER READING			TOTAL MILES	
		From	To	Start	End	Distance (km)	Business	Private

Daily checks	Tires/ Wheel	Wipers	Lights	Mirrors	Horn	Seatbelts	Brakes	Coupling devices
Monday								
Tuesday								
Wednesday								
Thursday								
Friday								
Saturday								
Sunday								

Fuel Input				
Date	Quantity	Unit	Mileage	Units

Notes :

Signature :

Vehicle Mileage Logbook

Sheet no.:

Make : | Model : | Year : | License number :

DATE	PURPOSE OF TRAVEL	JOURNEY		ODOMETER READING			TOTAL MILES	
		From	To	Start	End	Distance (km)	Business	Private

Daily checks	Tires/ Wheel	Wipers	Lights	Mirrors	Horn	Seatbelts	Brakes	Coupling devices
Monday								
Tuesday								
Wednesday								
Thursday								
Friday								
Saturday								
Sunday								

Fuel Input				
Date	Quantity	Unit	Mileage	Units

Notes :

Signature :

Vehicle Mileage Logbook

Sheet no.:

Make :	Model :	Year :	License number :

DATE	PURPOSE OF TRAVEL	JOURNEY		ODOMETER READING			TOTAL MILES	
		From	To	Start	End	Distance (km)	Business	Private

Daily checks	Tires/ Wheel	Wipers	Lights	Mirrors	Horn	Seatbelts	Brakes	Coupling devices
Monday								
Tuesday								
Wednesday								
Thursday								
Friday								
Saturday								
Sunday								

Fuel Input				
Date	Quantity	Unit	Mileage	Units

Notes :

Signature :

Vehicle Mileage Logbook

Sheet no.:

Make :	Model :	Year :	License number :

DATE	PURPOSE OF TRAVEL	JOURNEY		ODOMETER READING			TOTAL MILES	
		From	To	Start	End	Distance (km)	Business	Private

Daily checks	Tires/ Wheel	Wipers	Lights	Mirrors	Horn	Seatbelts	Brakes	Coupling devices
Monday								
Tuesday								
Wednesday								
Thursday								
Friday								
Saturday								
Sunday								

Fuel Input				
Date	Quantity	Unit	Mileage	Units

Notes :

Signature :

Vehicle Mileage Logbook

Sheet no.:

Make :	Model :	Year :	License number :

DATE	PURPOSE OF TRAVEL	JOURNEY		ODOMETER READING			TOTAL MILES	
		From	To	Start	End	Distance (km)	Business	Private

Daily checks	Tires/ Wheel	Wipers	Lights	Mirrors	Horn	Seatbelts	Brakes	Coupling devices
Monday								
Tuesday								
Wednesday								
Thursday								
Friday								
Saturday								
Sunday								

Fuel Input				
Date	Quantity	Unit	Mileage	Units

Notes :

Signature :

Vehicle Mileage Logbook

Sheet no.:

Make : | Model : | Year : | License number :

DATE	PURPOSE OF TRAVEL	JOURNEY		ODOMETER READING			TOTAL MILES	
		From	To	Start	End	Distance (km)	Business	Private

Daily checks	Tires/ Wheel	Wipers	Lights	Mirrors	Horn	Seatbelts	Brakes	Coupling devices
Monday								
Tuesday								
Wednesday								
Thursday								
Friday								
Saturday								
Sunday								

Fuel Input				
Date	Quantity	Unit	Mileage	Units

Notes :

Signature :

Vehicle Mileage Logbook

Sheet no.:

Make :	Model :	Year :	License number :

DATE	PURPOSE OF TRAVEL	JOURNEY		ODOMETER READING			TOTAL MILES	
		From	To	Start	End	Distance (km)	Business	Private

Daily checks	Tires/ Wheel	Wipers	Lights	Mirrors	Horn	Seatbelts	Brakes	Coupling devices
Monday								
Tuesday								
Wednesday								
Thursday								
Friday								
Saturday								
Sunday								

Fuel Input				
Date	Quantity	Unit	Mileage	Units

Notes :

Signature :

Vehicle Mileage Logbook

Sheet no.:

Make : | Model : | Year : | License number :

DATE	PURPOSE OF TRAVEL	JOURNEY		ODOMETER READING			TOTAL MILES	
		From	To	Start	End	Distance (km)	Business	Private

Daily checks	Tires/ Wheel	Wipers	Lights	Mirrors	Horn	Seatbelts	Brakes	Coupling devices
Monday								
Tuesday								
Wednesday								
Thursday								
Friday								
Saturday								
Sunday								

Fuel Input				
Date	Quantity	Unit	Mileage	Units

Notes :

Signature :

Vehicle Mileage Logbook

Sheet no.:

Make :	Model :	Year :	License number :

DATE	PURPOSE OF TRAVEL	JOURNEY		ODOMETER READING			TOTAL MILES	
		From	To	Start	End	Distance (km)	Business	Private

Daily checks	Tires/ Wheel	Wipers	Lights	Mirrors	Horn	Seatbelts	Brakes	Coupling devices
Monday								
Tuesday								
Wednesday								
Thursday								
Friday								
Saturday								
Sunday								

Fuel Input				
Date	Quantity	Unit	Mileage	Units

Notes :

Signature :

Vehicle Mileage Logbook

Sheet no.:

Make :	Model :	Year :	License number :

DATE	PURPOSE OF TRAVEL	JOURNEY		ODOMETER READING			TOTAL MILES	
		From	To	Start	End	Distance (km)	Business	Private

Daily checks	Tires/ Wheel	Wipers	Lights	Mirrors	Horn	Seatbelts	Brakes	Coupling devices
Monday								
Tuesday								
Wednesday								
Thursday								
Friday								
Saturday								
Sunday								

Fuel Input				
Date	Quantity	Unit	Mileage	Units

Notes :

____

____

____

____

____

____

____

Signature :

Vehicle Mileage Logbook

Sheet no.:

Make :	Model :	Year :	License number :

DATE	PURPOSE OF TRAVEL	JOURNEY		ODOMETER READING			TOTAL MILES	
		From	To	Start	End	Distance (km)	Business	Private

Daily checks	Tires/ Wheel	Wipers	Lights	Mirrors	Horn	Seatbelts	Brakes	Coupling devices
Monday								
Tuesday								
Wednesday								
Thursday								
Friday								
Saturday								
Sunday								

Fuel Input				
Date	Quantity	Unit	Mileage	Units

Notes :

Signature :

Vehicle Mileage Logbook

Vehicle Mileage Logbook	Sheet no.:

Make :	Model :	Year :	License number :

DATE	PURPOSE OF TRAVEL	JOURNEY		ODOMETER READING			TOTAL MILES	
		From	To	Start	End	Distance (km)	Business	Private

Daily checks	Tires/ Wheel	Wipers	Lights	Mirrors	Horn	Seatbelts	Brakes	Coupling devices
Monday								
Tuesday								
Wednesday								
Thursday								
Friday								
Saturday								
Sunday								

Fuel Input				
Date	Quantity	Unit	Mileage	Units

Notes :

Signature :

Vehicle Mileage Logbook

Sheet no.:

Make :	Model :	Year :	License number :

DATE	PURPOSE OF TRAVEL	JOURNEY		ODOMETER READING			TOTAL MILES	
		From	To	Start	End	Distance (km)	Business	Private

Daily checks	Tires/ Wheel	Wipers	Lights	Mirrors	Horn	Seatbelts	Brakes	Coupling devices
Monday								
Tuesday								
Wednesday								
Thursday								
Friday								
Saturday								
Sunday								

Fuel Input				
Date	Quantity	Unit	Mileage	Units

Notes :

Signature :

Vehicle Mileage Logbook

Sheet no.:

Make :	Model :	Year :	License number :

DATE	PURPOSE OF TRAVEL	JOURNEY		ODOMETER READING			TOTAL MILES	
		From	To	Start	End	Distance (km)	Business	Private

Daily checks	Tires/ Wheel	Wipers	Lights	Mirrors	Horn	Seatbelts	Brakes	Coupling devices
Monday								
Tuesday								
Wednesday								
Thursday								
Friday								
Saturday								
Sunday								

Fuel Input				
Date	Quantity	Unit	Mileage	Units

Notes :

Signature :

Vehicle Mileage Logbook

Sheet no.:

Make :	Model :	Year :	License number :

DATE	PURPOSE OF TRAVEL	JOURNEY		ODOMETER READING			TOTAL MILES	
		From	To	Start	End	Distance (km)	Business	Private

Daily checks	Tires/ Wheel	Wipers	Lights	Mirrors	Horn	Seatbelts	Brakes	Coupling devices
Monday								
Tuesday								
Wednesday								
Thursday								
Friday								
Saturday								
Sunday								

Fuel Input				
Date	Quantity	Unit	Mileage	Units

Notes :

Signature :

Vehicle Mileage Logbook

Sheet no.:

Make :	Model :	Year :	License number :

DATE	PURPOSE OF TRAVEL	JOURNEY		ODOMETER READING			TOTAL MILES	
		From	To	Start	End	Distance (km)	Business	Private

Daily checks	Tires/ Wheel	Wipers	Lights	Mirrors	Horn	Seatbelts	Brakes	Coupling devices
Monday								
Tuesday								
Wednesday								
Thursday								
Friday								
Saturday								
Sunday								

Fuel Input				
Date	Quantity	Unit	Mileage	Units

Notes :

Signature :

Vehicle Mileage Logbook

Sheet no.:

Make :	Model :	Year :	License number :

DATE	PURPOSE OF TRAVEL	JOURNEY		ODOMETER READING			TOTAL MILES	
		From	To	Start	End	Distance (km)	Business	Private

Daily checks	Tires/ Wheel	Wipers	Lights	Mirrors	Horn	Seatbelts	Brakes	Coupling devices
Monday								
Tuesday								
Wednesday								
Thursday								
Friday								
Saturday								
Sunday								

Fuel Input				
Date	Quantity	Unit	Mileage	Units

Notes :

Signature :

Vehicle Mileage Logbook

Sheet no.:

Make : | Model : | Year : | License number :

DATE	PURPOSE OF TRAVEL	JOURNEY		ODOMETER READING			TOTAL MILES	
		From	To	Start	End	Distance (km)	Business	Private

Daily checks	Tires/ Wheel	Wipers	Lights	Mirrors	Horn	Seatbelts	Brakes	Coupling devices
Monday								
Tuesday								
Wednesday								
Thursday								
Friday								
Saturday								
Sunday								

Fuel Input				
Date	Quantity	Unit	Mileage	Units

Notes :

Signature :

Vehicle Mileage Logbook

Sheet no.:

Make :	Model :	Year :	License number :

DATE	PURPOSE OF TRAVEL	JOURNEY		ODOMETER READING			TOTAL MILES	
		From	To	Start	End	Distance (km)	Business	Private

Daily checks	Tires/ Wheel	Wipers	Lights	Mirrors	Horn	Seatbelts	Brakes	Coupling devices
Monday								
Tuesday								
Wednesday								
Thursday								
Friday								
Saturday								
Sunday								

Fuel Input				
Date	Quantity	Unit	Mileage	Units

Notes :

Signature :

Vehicle Mileage Logbook

Vehicle Mileage Logbook	Sheet no.:

Make :	Model :	Year :	License number :

DATE	PURPOSE OF TRAVEL	JOURNEY		ODOMETER READING			TOTAL MILES	
		From	To	Start	End	Distance (km)	Business	Private

Daily checks	Tires/ Wheel	Wipers	Lights	Mirrors	Horn	Seatbelts	Brakes	Coupling devices
Monday								
Tuesday								
Wednesday								
Thursday								
Friday								
Saturday								
Sunday								

Fuel Input				
Date	Quantity	Unit	Mileage	Units

Notes :

Signature :

Vehicle Mileage Logbook

Sheet no.:

Make :	Model :	Year :	License number :

DATE	PURPOSE OF TRAVEL	JOURNEY		ODOMETER READING			TOTAL MILES	
		From	To	Start	End	Distance (km)	Business	Private

Daily checks	Tires/ Wheel	Wipers	Lights	Mirrors	Horn	Seatbelts	Brakes	Coupling devices
Monday								
Tuesday								
Wednesday								
Thursday								
Friday								
Saturday								
Sunday								

Fuel Input				
Date	Quantity	Unit	Mileage	Units

Notes :

Signature :

Vehicle Mileage Logbook

Sheet no.:

Make :	Model :	Year :	License number :

DATE	PURPOSE OF TRAVEL	JOURNEY		ODOMETER READING			TOTAL MILES	
		From	To	Start	End	Distance (km)	Business	Private

Daily checks	Tires/ Wheel	Wipers	Lights	Mirrors	Horn	Seatbelts	Brakes	Coupling devices
Monday								
Tuesday								
Wednesday								
Thursday								
Friday								
Saturday								
Sunday								

Fuel Input				
Date	Quantity	Unit	Mileage	Units

Notes :

Signature :

Vehicle Mileage Logbook

Sheet no.:

Make :	Model :	Year :	License number :

DATE	PURPOSE OF TRAVEL	JOURNEY		ODOMETER READING			TOTAL MILES	
		From	To	Start	End	Distance (km)	Business	Private

Daily checks	Tires/ Wheel	Wipers	Lights	Mirrors	Horn	Seatbelts	Brakes	Coupling devices
Monday								
Tuesday								
Wednesday								
Thursday								
Friday								
Saturday								
Sunday								

Fuel Input				
Date	Quantity	Unit	Mileage	Units

Notes :

Signature :

Vehicle Mileage Logbook

Sheet no.:

Make :	Model :	Year :	License number :

DATE	PURPOSE OF TRAVEL	JOURNEY		ODOMETER READING			TOTAL MILES	
		From	To	Start	End	Distance (km)	Business	Private

Daily checks	Tires/ Wheel	Wipers	Lights	Mirrors	Horn	Seatbelts	Brakes	Coupling devices
Monday								
Tuesday								
Wednesday								
Thursday								
Friday								
Saturday								
Sunday								

Fuel Input				
Date	Quantity	Unit	Mileage	Units

Notes :

Signature :

Vehicle Mileage Logbook

Sheet no.:

Make :	Model :	Year :	License number :

DATE	PURPOSE OF TRAVEL	JOURNEY		ODOMETER READING			TOTAL MILES	
		From	To	Start	End	Distance (km)	Business	Private

Daily checks	Tires/ Wheel	Wipers	Lights	Mirrors	Horn	Seatbelts	Brakes	Coupling devices
Monday								
Tuesday								
Wednesday								
Thursday								
Friday								
Saturday								
Sunday								

Fuel Input				
Date	Quantity	Unit	Mileage	Units

Notes :

Signature :

Vehicle Mileage Logbook

Sheet no.:

Make :	Model :	Year :	License number :

DATE	PURPOSE OF TRAVEL	JOURNEY		ODOMETER READING			TOTAL MILES	
		From	To	Start	End	Distance (km)	Business	Private

Daily checks	Tires/ Wheel	Wipers	Lights	Mirrors	Horn	Seatbelts	Brakes	Coupling devices
Monday								
Tuesday								
Wednesday								
Thursday								
Friday								
Saturday								
Sunday								

Fuel Input				
Date	Quantity	Unit	Mileage	Units

Notes :

Signature :

Vehicle Mileage Logbook

Sheet no.:

Make :	Model :	Year :	License number :

DATE	PURPOSE OF TRAVEL	JOURNEY		ODOMETER READING			TOTAL MILES	
		From	To	Start	End	Distance (km)	Business	Private

Daily checks	Tires/ Wheel	Wipers	Lights	Mirrors	Horn	Seatbelts	Brakes	Coupling devices
Monday								
Tuesday								
Wednesday								
Thursday								
Friday								
Saturday								
Sunday								

Fuel Input				
Date	Quantity	Unit	Mileage	Units

Notes :

Signature :

Vehicle Mileage Logbook

Vehicle Mileage Logbook			Sheet no.:
Make :	Model :	Year :	License number :

DATE	PURPOSE OF TRAVEL	JOURNEY		ODOMETER READING			TOTAL MILES	
		From	To	Start	End	Distance (km)	Business	Private

Daily checks	Tires/ Wheel	Wipers	Lights	Mirrors	Horn	Seatbelts	Brakes	Coupling devices
Monday								
Tuesday								
Wednesday								
Thursday								
Friday								
Saturday								
Sunday								

Fuel Input				
Date	Quantity	Unit	Mileage	Units

Notes :

Signature :

Vehicle Mileage Logbook

Sheet no.:

Make :	Model :	Year :	License number :

DATE	PURPOSE OF TRAVEL	JOURNEY		ODOMETER READING			TOTAL MILES	
		From	To	Start	End	Distance (km)	Business	Private

Daily checks	Tires/ Wheel	Wipers	Lights	Mirrors	Horn	Seatbelts	Brakes	Coupling devices
Monday								
Tuesday								
Wednesday								
Thursday								
Friday								
Saturday								
Sunday								

Fuel Input				
Date	Quantity	Unit	Mileage	Units

Notes :

Signature :

Vehicle Mileage Logbook

Vehicle Mileage Logbook	Sheet no.:

Make :	Model :	Year :	License number :

DATE	PURPOSE OF TRAVEL	JOURNEY		ODOMETER READING			TOTAL MILES	
		From	To	Start	End	Distance (km)	Business	Private

Daily checks	Tires/ Wheel	Wipers	Lights	Mirrors	Horn	Seatbelts	Brakes	Coupling devices
Monday								
Tuesday								
Wednesday								
Thursday								
Friday								
Saturday								
Sunday								

Fuel Input				
Date	Quantity	Unit	Mileage	Units

Notes :

Signature :

Vehicle Mileage Logbook

Sheet no.:

Make :	Model :	Year :	License number :

DATE	PURPOSE OF TRAVEL	JOURNEY		ODOMETER READING			TOTAL MILES	
		From	To	Start	End	Distance (km)	Business	Private

Daily checks	Tires/ Wheel	Wipers	Lights	Mirrors	Horn	Seatbelts	Brakes	Coupling devices
Monday								
Tuesday								
Wednesday								
Thursday								
Friday								
Saturday								
Sunday								

Fuel Input				
Date	Quantity	Unit	Mileage	Units

Notes :

Signature :

Vehicle Mileage Logbook

Sheet no.:

Make :	Model :	Year :	License number :

DATE	PURPOSE OF TRAVEL	JOURNEY		ODOMETER READING			TOTAL MILES	
		From	To	Start	End	Distance (km)	Business	Private

Daily checks	Tires/ Wheel	Wipers	Lights	Mirrors	Horn	Seatbelts	Brakes	Coupling devices
Monday								
Tuesday								
Wednesday								
Thursday								
Friday								
Saturday								
Sunday								

Fuel Input				
Date	Quantity	Unit	Mileage	Units

Notes :

Signature :

Vehicle Mileage Logbook

Vehicle Mileage Logbook			Sheet no.:
Make :	Model :	Year :	License number :

DATE	PURPOSE OF TRAVEL	JOURNEY		ODOMETER READING			TOTAL MILES	
		From	To	Start	End	Distance (km)	Business	Private

Daily checks	Tires/ Wheel	Wipers	Lights	Mirrors	Horn	Seatbelts	Brakes	Coupling devices
Monday								
Tuesday								
Wednesday								
Thursday								
Friday								
Saturday								
Sunday								

Fuel Input				
Date	Quantity	Unit	Mileage	Units

Notes :

Signature :

Vehicle Mileage Logbook

Sheet no.:

Make : | Model : | Year : | License number :

DATE	PURPOSE OF TRAVEL	JOURNEY		ODOMETER READING			TOTAL MILES	
		From	To	Start	End	Distance (km)	Business	Private

Daily checks	Tires/ Wheel	Wipers	Lights	Mirrors	Horn	Seatbelts	Brakes	Coupling devices
Monday								
Tuesday								
Wednesday								
Thursday								
Friday								
Saturday								
Sunday								

Fuel Input				
Date	Quantity	Unit	Mileage	Units

Notes :

Signature :

Vehicle Mileage Logbook

Sheet no.:

Make :	Model :	Year :	License number :

DATE	PURPOSE OF TRAVEL	JOURNEY		ODOMETER READING			TOTAL MILES	
		From	To	Start	End	Distance (km)	Business	Private

Daily checks	Tires/ Wheel	Wipers	Lights	Mirrors	Horn	Seatbelts	Brakes	Coupling devices
Monday								
Tuesday								
Wednesday								
Thursday								
Friday								
Saturday								
Sunday								

Fuel Input				
Date	Quantity	Unit	Mileage	Units

Notes :

Signature :

Vehicle Mileage Logbook

Sheet no.:

Make : | Model : | Year : | License number :

DATE	PURPOSE OF TRAVEL	JOURNEY		ODOMETER READING			TOTAL MILES	
		From	To	Start	End	Distance (km)	Business	Private

Daily checks	Tires/ Wheel	Wipers	Lights	Mirrors	Horn	Seatbelts	Brakes	Coupling devices
Monday								
Tuesday								
Wednesday								
Thursday								
Friday								
Saturday								
Sunday								

Fuel Input				
Date	Quantity	Unit	Mileage	Units

Notes :

Signature :

Vehicle Mileage Logbook

Sheet no.:

Make :	Model :	Year :	License number :

DATE	PURPOSE OF TRAVEL	JOURNEY		ODOMETER READING			TOTAL MILES	
		From	To	Start	End	Distance (km)	Business	Private

Daily checks	Tires/ Wheel	Wipers	Lights	Mirrors	Horn	Seatbelts	Brakes	Coupling devices
Monday								
Tuesday								
Wednesday								
Thursday								
Friday								
Saturday								
Sunday								

Fuel Input				
Date	Quantity	Unit	Mileage	Units

Notes :

Signature :

Vehicle Mileage Logbook

Sheet no.:

Make :	Model :	Year :	License number :

DATE	PURPOSE OF TRAVEL	JOURNEY		ODOMETER READING			TOTAL MILES	
		From	To	Start	End	Distance (km)	Business	Private

Daily checks	Tires/ Wheel	Wipers	Lights	Mirrors	Horn	Seatbelts	Brakes	Coupling devices
Monday								
Tuesday								
Wednesday								
Thursday								
Friday								
Saturday								
Sunday								

Fuel Input				
Date	Quantity	Unit	Mileage	Units

Notes :

Signature :

Vehicle Mileage Logbook

Sheet no.:

Make :	Model :	Year :	License number :

DATE	PURPOSE OF TRAVEL	JOURNEY		ODOMETER READING			TOTAL MILES	
		From	To	Start	End	Distance (km)	Business	Private

Daily checks	Tires/ Wheel	Wipers	Lights	Mirrors	Horn	Seatbelts	Brakes	Coupling devices
Monday								
Tuesday								
Wednesday								
Thursday								
Friday								
Saturday								
Sunday								

Fuel Input				
Date	Quantity	Unit	Mileage	Units

Notes :

Signature :

Vehicle Mileage Logbook

Vehicle Mileage Logbook	Sheet no.:

Make :	Model :	Year :	License number :

DATE	PURPOSE OF TRAVEL	JOURNEY		ODOMETER READING			TOTAL MILES	
		From	To	Start	End	Distance (km)	Business	Private

Daily checks	Tires/ Wheel	Wipers	Lights	Mirrors	Horn	Seatbelts	Brakes	Coupling devices
Monday								
Tuesday								
Wednesday								
Thursday								
Friday								
Saturday								
Sunday								

Fuel Input				
Date	Quantity	Unit	Mileage	Units

Notes :

Signature :

Vehicle Mileage Logbook

Vehicle Mileage Logbook	Sheet no.:

Make :	Model :	Year :	License number :

DATE	PURPOSE OF TRAVEL	JOURNEY		ODOMETER READING			TOTAL MILES	
		From	To	Start	End	Distance (km)	Business	Private

Daily checks	Tires/ Wheel	Wipers	Lights	Mirrors	Horn	Seatbelts	Brakes	Coupling devices
Monday								
Tuesday								
Wednesday								
Thursday								
Friday								
Saturday								
Sunday								

Fuel Input				
Date	Quantity	Unit	Mileage	Units

Notes :

Signature :

Vehicle Mileage Logbook

Sheet no.:

Make : | Model : | Year : | License number :

DATE	PURPOSE OF TRAVEL	JOURNEY		ODOMETER READING			TOTAL MILES	
		From	To	Start	End	Distance (km)	Business	Private

Daily checks	Tires/ Wheel	Wipers	Lights	Mirrors	Horn	Seatbelts	Brakes	Coupling devices
Monday								
Tuesday								
Wednesday								
Thursday								
Friday								
Saturday								
Sunday								

Fuel Input				
Date	Quantity	Unit	Mileage	Units

Notes :

Signature :

Vehicle Mileage Logbook

Sheet no.:

Make : | Model : | Year : | License number :

DATE	PURPOSE OF TRAVEL	JOURNEY		ODOMETER READING			TOTAL MILES	
		From	To	Start	End	Distance (km)	Business	Private

Daily checks	Tires/ Wheel	Wipers	Lights	Mirrors	Horn	Seatbelts	Brakes	Coupling devices
Monday								
Tuesday								
Wednesday								
Thursday								
Friday								
Saturday								
Sunday								

Fuel Input				
Date	Quantity	Unit	Mileage	Units

Notes :

Signature :

Vehicle Mileage Logbook

Sheet no.:

Make :	Model :	Year :	License number :

DATE	PURPOSE OF TRAVEL	JOURNEY		ODOMETER READING			TOTAL MILES	
		From	To	Start	End	Distance (km)	Business	Private

Daily checks	Tires/ Wheel	Wipers	Lights	Mirrors	Horn	Seatbelts	Brakes	Coupling devices
Monday								
Tuesday								
Wednesday								
Thursday								
Friday								
Saturday								
Sunday								

Fuel Input				
Date	Quantity	Unit	Mileage	Units

Notes :

Signature :

Vehicle Mileage Logbook

Sheet no.:

Make :	Model :	Year :	License number :

DATE	PURPOSE OF TRAVEL	JOURNEY		ODOMETER READING			TOTAL MILES	
		From	To	Start	End	Distance (km)	Business	Private

Daily checks	Tires/ Wheel	Wipers	Lights	Mirrors	Horn	Seatbelts	Brakes	Coupling devices
Monday								
Tuesday								
Wednesday								
Thursday								
Friday								
Saturday								
Sunday								

Fuel Input				
Date	Quantity	Unit	Mileage	Units

Notes :

Signature :

Vehicle Mileage Logbook

Vehicle Mileage Logbook	Sheet no.:

Make :	Model :	Year :	License number :

DATE	PURPOSE OF TRAVEL	JOURNEY		ODOMETER READING			TOTAL MILES	
		From	To	Start	End	Distance (km)	Business	Private

Daily checks	Tires/ Wheel	Wipers	Lights	Mirrors	Horn	Seatbelts	Brakes	Coupling devices
Monday								
Tuesday								
Wednesday								
Thursday								
Friday								
Saturday								
Sunday								

Fuel Input				
Date	Quantity	Unit	Mileage	Units

Notes :

Signature :

Vehicle Mileage Logbook

Sheet no.:

Make :	Model :	Year :	License number :

DATE	PURPOSE OF TRAVEL	JOURNEY		ODOMETER READING			TOTAL MILES	
		From	To	Start	End	Distance (km)	Business	Private

Daily checks	Tires/ Wheel	Wipers	Lights	Mirrors	Horn	Seatbelts	Brakes	Coupling devices
Monday								
Tuesday								
Wednesday								
Thursday								
Friday								
Saturday								
Sunday								

Fuel Input				
Date	Quantity	Unit	Mileage	Units

Notes :

Signature :

Vehicle Mileage Logbook

Sheet no.:

Make :	Model :	Year :	License number :

DATE	PURPOSE OF TRAVEL	JOURNEY		ODOMETER READING			TOTAL MILES	
		From	To	Start	End	Distance (km)	Business	Private

Daily checks	Tires/ Wheel	Wipers	Lights	Mirrors	Horn	Seatbelts	Brakes	Coupling devices
Monday								
Tuesday								
Wednesday								
Thursday								
Friday								
Saturday								
Sunday								

Fuel Input				
Date	Quantity	Unit	Mileage	Units

Notes :

Signature :

Vehicle Mileage Logbook

Sheet no.:

Make :	Model :	Year :	License number :

DATE	PURPOSE OF TRAVEL	JOURNEY		ODOMETER READING			TOTAL MILES	
		From	To	Start	End	Distance (km)	Business	Private

Daily checks	Tires/ Wheel	Wipers	Lights	Mirrors	Horn	Seatbelts	Brakes	Coupling devices
Monday								
Tuesday								
Wednesday								
Thursday								
Friday								
Saturday								
Sunday								

Fuel Input				
Date	Quantity	Unit	Mileage	Units

Notes :

Signature :

Vehicle Mileage Logbook

Sheet no.:

Make :	Model :	Year :	License number :

DATE	PURPOSE OF TRAVEL	JOURNEY		ODOMETER READING			TOTAL MILES	
		From	To	Start	End	Distance (km)	Business	Private

Daily checks	Tires/ Wheel	Wipers	Lights	Mirrors	Horn	Seatbelts	Brakes	Coupling devices
Monday								
Tuesday								
Wednesday								
Thursday								
Friday								
Saturday								
Sunday								

Fuel Input				
Date	Quantity	Unit	Mileage	Units

Notes :

Signature :

Vehicle Mileage Logbook

Sheet no.:

Make :	Model :	Year :	License number :

DATE	PURPOSE OF TRAVEL	JOURNEY		ODOMETER READING			TOTAL MILES	
		From	To	Start	End	Distance (km)	Business	Private

Daily checks	Tires/ Wheel	Wipers	Lights	Mirrors	Horn	Seatbelts	Brakes	Coupling devices
Monday								
Tuesday								
Wednesday								
Thursday								
Friday								
Saturday								
Sunday								

Fuel Input				
Date	Quantity	Unit	Mileage	Units

Notes :

Signature :

Vehicle Mileage Logbook

Vehicle Mileage Logbook	Sheet no.:

Make :	Model :	Year :	License number :

DATE	PURPOSE OF TRAVEL	JOURNEY		ODOMETER READING			TOTAL MILES	
		From	To	Start	End	Distance (km)	Business	Private

Daily checks	Tires/ Wheel	Wipers	Lights	Mirrors	Horn	Seatbelts	Brakes	Coupling devices
Monday								
Tuesday								
Wednesday								
Thursday								
Friday								
Saturday								
Sunday								

Fuel Input				
Date	Quantity	Unit	Mileage	Units

Notes :

Signature :

Vehicle Mileage Logbook

Make :	Model :	Year :	License number :	Sheet no.:

DATE	PURPOSE OF TRAVEL	JOURNEY		ODOMETER READING			TOTAL MILES	
		From	To	Start	End	Distance (km)	Business	Private

Daily checks	Tires/ Wheel	Wipers	Lights	Mirrors	Horn	Seatbelts	Brakes	Coupling devices
Monday								
Tuesday								
Wednesday								
Thursday								
Friday								
Saturday								
Sunday								

Fuel Input				
Date	Quantity	Unit	Mileage	Units

Notes :

Signature :

Vehicle Mileage Logbook

Sheet no.:

Make :	Model :	Year :	License number :

DATE	PURPOSE OF TRAVEL	JOURNEY		ODOMETER READING			TOTAL MILES	
		From	To	Start	End	Distance (km)	Business	Private

Daily checks	Tires/ Wheel	Wipers	Lights	Mirrors	Horn	Seatbelts	Brakes	Coupling devices
Monday								
Tuesday								
Wednesday								
Thursday								
Friday								
Saturday								
Sunday								

Fuel Input				
Date	Quantity	Unit	Mileage	Units

Notes :

Signature :

Vehicle Mileage Logbook

Sheet no.:

Make :	Model :	Year :	License number :

DATE	PURPOSE OF TRAVEL	JOURNEY		ODOMETER READING			TOTAL MILES	
		From	To	Start	End	Distance (km)	Business	Private

Daily checks	Tires/ Wheel	Wipers	Lights	Mirrors	Horn	Seatbelts	Brakes	Coupling devices
Monday								
Tuesday								
Wednesday								
Thursday								
Friday								
Saturday								
Sunday								

Fuel Input				
Date	Quantity	Unit	Mileage	Units

Notes :

Signature :

Vehicle Mileage Logbook

Sheet no.:

Make :	Model :	Year :	License number :

DATE	PURPOSE OF TRAVEL	JOURNEY		ODOMETER READING			TOTAL MILES	
		From	To	Start	End	Distance (km)	Business	Private

Daily checks	Tires/ Wheel	Wipers	Lights	Mirrors	Horn	Seatbelts	Brakes	Coupling devices
Monday								
Tuesday								
Wednesday								
Thursday								
Friday								
Saturday								
Sunday								

Fuel Input				
Date	Quantity	Unit	Mileage	Units

Notes :

Signature :

Vehicle Mileage Logbook

Sheet no.:

Make :	Model :	Year :	License number :

DATE	PURPOSE OF TRAVEL	JOURNEY		ODOMETER READING			TOTAL MILES	
		From	To	Start	End	Distance (km)	Business	Private

Daily checks	Tires/ Wheel	Wipers	Lights	Mirrors	Horn	Seatbelts	Brakes	Coupling devices
Monday								
Tuesday								
Wednesday								
Thursday								
Friday								
Saturday								
Sunday								

Fuel Input				
Date	Quantity	Unit	Mileage	Units

Notes :

Signature :

Vehicle Mileage Logbook

Sheet no.:

Make :	Model :	Year :	License number :

DATE	PURPOSE OF TRAVEL	JOURNEY		ODOMETER READING			TOTAL MILES	
		From	To	Start	End	Distance (km)	Business	Private

Daily checks	Tires/ Wheel	Wipers	Lights	Mirrors	Horn	Seatbelts	Brakes	Coupling devices
Monday								
Tuesday								
Wednesday								
Thursday								
Friday								
Saturday								
Sunday								

Fuel Input				
Date	Quantity	Unit	Mileage	Units

Notes :

Signature :

Vehicle Mileage Logbook

Sheet no.:

Make :	Model :	Year :	License number :

DATE	PURPOSE OF TRAVEL	JOURNEY		ODOMETER READING			TOTAL MILES	
		From	To	Start	End	Distance (km)	Business	Private

Daily checks	Tires/ Wheel	Wipers	Lights	Mirrors	Horn	Seatbelts	Brakes	Coupling devices
Monday								
Tuesday								
Wednesday								
Thursday								
Friday								
Saturday								
Sunday								

Fuel Input				
Date	Quantity	Unit	Mileage	Units

Notes :

Signature :

Vehicle Mileage Logbook

Sheet no.:

Make :	Model :	Year :	License number :

DATE	PURPOSE OF TRAVEL	JOURNEY		ODOMETER READING			TOTAL MILES	
		From	To	Start	End	Distance (km)	Business	Private

Daily checks	Tires/ Wheel	Wipers	Lights	Mirrors	Horn	Seatbelts	Brakes	Coupling devices
Monday								
Tuesday								
Wednesday								
Thursday								
Friday								
Saturday								
Sunday								

Fuel Input				
Date	Quantity	Unit	Mileage	Units

Notes :

Signature :

Vehicle Mileage Logbook

Vehicle Mileage Logbook	Sheet no.:

Make :	Model :	Year :	License number :

DATE	PURPOSE OF TRAVEL	JOURNEY		ODOMETER READING			TOTAL MILES	
		From	To	Start	End	Distance (km)	Business	Private

Daily checks	Tires/ Wheel	Wipers	Lights	Mirrors	Horn	Seatbelts	Brakes	Coupling devices
Monday								
Tuesday								
Wednesday								
Thursday								
Friday								
Saturday								
Sunday								

Fuel Input				
Date	Quantity	Unit	Mileage	Units

Notes :

Signature :

Vehicle Mileage Logbook

Sheet no.:

Make :	Model :	Year :	License number :

DATE	PURPOSE OF TRAVEL	JOURNEY		ODOMETER READING			TOTAL MILES	
		From	To	Start	End	Distance (km)	Business	Private

Daily checks	Tires/ Wheel	Wipers	Lights	Mirrors	Horn	Seatbelts	Brakes	Coupling devices
Monday								
Tuesday								
Wednesday								
Thursday								
Friday								
Saturday								
Sunday								

Fuel Input				
Date	Quantity	Unit	Mileage	Units

Notes :

Signature :

Vehicle Mileage Logbook

Sheet no.:

Make :	Model :	Year :	License number :

DATE	PURPOSE OF TRAVEL	JOURNEY		ODOMETER READING			TOTAL MILES	
		From	To	Start	End	Distance (km)	Business	Private

Daily checks	Tires/ Wheel	Wipers	Lights	Mirrors	Horn	Seatbelts	Brakes	Coupling devices
Monday								
Tuesday								
Wednesday								
Thursday								
Friday								
Saturday								
Sunday								

Fuel Input				
Date	Quantity	Unit	Mileage	Units

Notes :

Signature :

Vehicle Mileage Logbook

Sheet no.:

Make :	Model :	Year :	License number :

DATE	PURPOSE OF TRAVEL	JOURNEY		ODOMETER READING			TOTAL MILES	
		From	To	Start	End	Distance (km)	Business	Private

Daily checks	Tires/ Wheel	Wipers	Lights	Mirrors	Horn	Seatbelts	Brakes	Coupling devices
Monday								
Tuesday								
Wednesday								
Thursday								
Friday								
Saturday								
Sunday								

Fuel Input				
Date	Quantity	Unit	Mileage	Units

Notes :

Signature :

Vehicle Mileage Logbook

Sheet no.:

Make :	Model :	Year :	License number :

DATE	PURPOSE OF TRAVEL	JOURNEY		ODOMETER READING			TOTAL MILES	
		From	To	Start	End	Distance (km)	Business	Private

Daily checks	Tires/ Wheel	Wipers	Lights	Mirrors	Horn	Seatbelts	Brakes	Coupling devices
Monday								
Tuesday								
Wednesday								
Thursday								
Friday								
Saturday								
Sunday								

Fuel Input				
Date	Quantity	Unit	Mileage	Units

Notes :

Signature :

Vehicle Mileage Logbook

Sheet no.:

Make :	Model :	Year :	License number :

DATE	PURPOSE OF TRAVEL	JOURNEY		ODOMETER READING			TOTAL MILES	
		From	To	Start	End	Distance (km)	Business	Private

Daily checks	Tires/ Wheel	Wipers	Lights	Mirrors	Horn	Seatbelts	Brakes	Coupling devices
Monday								
Tuesday								
Wednesday								
Thursday								
Friday								
Saturday								
Sunday								

Fuel Input				
Date	Quantity	Unit	Mileage	Units

Notes :

Signature :

Vehicle Mileage Logbook

Sheet no.:

Make :	Model :	Year :	License number :

DATE	PURPOSE OF TRAVEL	JOURNEY		ODOMETER READING			TOTAL MILES	
		From	To	Start	End	Distance (km)	Business	Private

Daily checks	Tires/ Wheel	Wipers	Lights	Mirrors	Horn	Seatbelts	Brakes	Coupling devices
Monday								
Tuesday								
Wednesday								
Thursday								
Friday								
Saturday								
Sunday								

Fuel Input				
Date	Quantity	Unit	Mileage	Units

Notes :

Signature :

Vehicle Mileage Logbook

Sheet no.:

Make :	Model :	Year :	License number :

DATE	PURPOSE OF TRAVEL	JOURNEY		ODOMETER READING			TOTAL MILES	
		From	To	Start	End	Distance (km)	Business	Private

Daily checks	Tires/ Wheel	Wipers	Lights	Mirrors	Horn	Seatbelts	Brakes	Coupling devices
Monday								
Tuesday								
Wednesday								
Thursday								
Friday								
Saturday								
Sunday								

Fuel Input				
Date	Quantity	Unit	Mileage	Units

Notes :

Signature :

Vehicle Mileage Logbook

Sheet no.:

Make :	Model :	Year :	License number :

DATE	PURPOSE OF TRAVEL	JOURNEY		ODOMETER READING			TOTAL MILES	
		From	To	Start	End	Distance (km)	Business	Private

Daily checks	Tires/ Wheel	Wipers	Lights	Mirrors	Horn	Seatbelts	Brakes	Coupling devices
Monday								
Tuesday								
Wednesday								
Thursday								
Friday								
Saturday								
Sunday								

Fuel Input				
Date	Quantity	Unit	Mileage	Units

Notes :

Signature :

Vehicle Mileage Logbook

Sheet no.:

Make :	Model :	Year :	License number :

DATE	PURPOSE OF TRAVEL	JOURNEY		ODOMETER READING			TOTAL MILES	
		From	To	Start	End	Distance (km)	Business	Private

Daily checks	Tires/ Wheel	Wipers	Lights	Mirrors	Horn	Seatbelts	Brakes	Coupling devices
Monday								
Tuesday								
Wednesday								
Thursday								
Friday								
Saturday								
Sunday								

Fuel Input				
Date	Quantity	Unit	Mileage	Units

Notes :

Signature :

Vehicle Mileage Logbook

Sheet no.:

Make : | Model : | Year : | License number :

DATE	PURPOSE OF TRAVEL	JOURNEY		ODOMETER READING			TOTAL MILES	
		From	To	Start	End	Distance (km)	Business	Private

Daily checks	Tires/ Wheel	Wipers	Lights	Mirrors	Horn	Seatbelts	Brakes	Coupling devices
Monday								
Tuesday								
Wednesday								
Thursday								
Friday								
Saturday								
Sunday								

Fuel Input				
Date	Quantity	Unit	Mileage	Units

Notes :

Signature :

Vehicle Mileage Logbook

Sheet no.:

Make :	Model :	Year :	License number :

DATE	PURPOSE OF TRAVEL	JOURNEY		ODOMETER READING			TOTAL MILES	
		From	To	Start	End	Distance (km)	Business	Private

Daily checks	Tires/ Wheel	Wipers	Lights	Mirrors	Horn	Seatbelts	Brakes	Coupling devices
Monday								
Tuesday								
Wednesday								
Thursday								
Friday								
Saturday								
Sunday								

Fuel Input				
Date	Quantity	Unit	Mileage	Units

Notes :

Signature :

Vehicle Mileage Logbook

Sheet no.:

Make :	Model :	Year :	License number :

DATE	PURPOSE OF TRAVEL	JOURNEY		ODOMETER READING			TOTAL MILES	
		From	To	Start	End	Distance (km)	Business	Private

Daily checks	Tires/ Wheel	Wipers	Lights	Mirrors	Horn	Seatbelts	Brakes	Coupling devices
Monday								
Tuesday								
Wednesday								
Thursday								
Friday								
Saturday								
Sunday								

Fuel Input				
Date	Quantity	Unit	Mileage	Units

Notes :

Signature :

Vehicle Mileage Logbook

Sheet no.:

Make :	Model :	Year :	License number :

DATE	PURPOSE OF TRAVEL	JOURNEY		ODOMETER READING			TOTAL MILES	
		From	To	Start	End	Distance (km)	Business	Private

Daily checks	Tires/ Wheel	Wipers	Lights	Mirrors	Horn	Seatbelts	Brakes	Coupling devices
Monday								
Tuesday								
Wednesday								
Thursday								
Friday								
Saturday								
Sunday								

Fuel Input				
Date	Quantity	Unit	Mileage	Units

Notes :

Signature :

Vehicle Mileage Logbook

Sheet no.:

Make :	Model :	Year :	License number :

DATE	PURPOSE OF TRAVEL	JOURNEY		ODOMETER READING			TOTAL MILES	
		From	To	Start	End	Distance (km)	Business	Private

Daily checks	Tires/ Wheel	Wipers	Lights	Mirrors	Horn	Seatbelts	Brakes	Coupling devices
Monday								
Tuesday								
Wednesday								
Thursday								
Friday								
Saturday								
Sunday								

Fuel Input				
Date	Quantity	Unit	Mileage	Units

Notes :

Signature :

Vehicle Mileage Logbook

Sheet no.:

Make :	Model :	Year :	License number :

DATE	PURPOSE OF TRAVEL	JOURNEY		ODOMETER READING			TOTAL MILES	
		From	To	Start	End	Distance (km)	Business	Private

Daily checks	Tires/ Wheel	Wipers	Lights	Mirrors	Horn	Seatbelts	Brakes	Coupling devices
Monday								
Tuesday								
Wednesday								
Thursday								
Friday								
Saturday								
Sunday								

Fuel Input				
Date	Quantity	Unit	Mileage	Units

Notes :

Signature :

Vehicle Mileage Logbook

Sheet no.:

Make :	Model :	Year :	License number :

DATE	PURPOSE OF TRAVEL	JOURNEY		ODOMETER READING			TOTAL MILES	
		From	To	Start	End	Distance (km)	Business	Private

Daily checks	Tires/ Wheel	Wipers	Lights	Mirrors	Horn	Seatbelts	Brakes	Coupling devices
Monday								
Tuesday								
Wednesday								
Thursday								
Friday								
Saturday								
Sunday								

Fuel Input				
Date	Quantity	Unit	Mileage	Units

Notes :

Signature :

Vehicle Mileage Logbook

Sheet no.:

Make : | Model : | Year : | License number :

DATE	PURPOSE OF TRAVEL	JOURNEY		ODOMETER READING			TOTAL MILES	
		From	To	Start	End	Distance (km)	Business	Private

Daily checks	Tires/ Wheel	Wipers	Lights	Mirrors	Horn	Seatbelts	Brakes	Coupling devices
Monday								
Tuesday								
Wednesday								
Thursday								
Friday								
Saturday								
Sunday								

Fuel Input				
Date	Quantity	Unit	Mileage	Units

Notes :

Signature :

Vehicle Mileage Logbook

Sheet no.:

Make :	Model :	Year :	License number :

DATE	PURPOSE OF TRAVEL	JOURNEY		ODOMETER READING			TOTAL MILES	
		From	To	Start	End	Distance (km)	Business	Private

Daily checks	Tires/ Wheel	Wipers	Lights	Mirrors	Horn	Seatbelts	Brakes	Coupling devices
Monday								
Tuesday								
Wednesday								
Thursday								
Friday								
Saturday								
Sunday								

Fuel Input				
Date	Quantity	Unit	Mileage	Units

Notes :

Signature :

Vehicle Mileage Logbook

Sheet no.:

Make : | Model : | Year : | License number :

DATE	PURPOSE OF TRAVEL	JOURNEY		ODOMETER READING			TOTAL MILES	
		From	To	Start	End	Distance (km)	Business	Private

Daily checks	Tires/ Wheel	Wipers	Lights	Mirrors	Horn	Seatbelts	Brakes	Coupling devices
Monday								
Tuesday								
Wednesday								
Thursday								
Friday								
Saturday								
Sunday								

Fuel Input				
Date	Quantity	Unit	Mileage	Units

Notes :

Signature :

Vehicle Mileage Logbook

Sheet no.:

Make :	Model :	Year :	License number :

DATE	PURPOSE OF TRAVEL	JOURNEY		ODOMETER READING			TOTAL MILES	
		From	To	Start	End	Distance (km)	Business	Private

Daily checks	Tires/ Wheel	Wipers	Lights	Mirrors	Horn	Seatbelts	Brakes	Coupling devices
Monday								
Tuesday								
Wednesday								
Thursday								
Friday								
Saturday								
Sunday								

Fuel Input				
Date	Quantity	Unit	Mileage	Units

Notes :

Signature :

Vehicle Mileage Logbook

Sheet no.:

Make : | Model : | Year : | License number :

DATE	PURPOSE OF TRAVEL	JOURNEY		ODOMETER READING			TOTAL MILES	
		From	To	Start	End	Distance (km)	Business	Private

Daily checks	Tires/ Wheel	Wipers	Lights	Mirrors	Horn	Seatbelts	Brakes	Coupling devices
Monday								
Tuesday								
Wednesday								
Thursday								
Friday								
Saturday								
Sunday								

Fuel Input				
Date	Quantity	Unit	Mileage	Units

Notes :

Signature :

Vehicle Mileage Logbook

Sheet no.:

Make :	Model :	Year :	License number :

DATE	PURPOSE OF TRAVEL	JOURNEY		ODOMETER READING			TOTAL MILES	
		From	To	Start	End	Distance (km)	Business	Private

Daily checks	Tires/ Wheel	Wipers	Lights	Mirrors	Horn	Seatbelts	Brakes	Coupling devices
Monday								
Tuesday								
Wednesday								
Thursday								
Friday								
Saturday								
Sunday								

Fuel Input				
Date	Quantity	Unit	Mileage	Units

Notes :

Signature :

Vehicle Mileage Logbook

Sheet no.:

Make :	Model :	Year :	License number :

DATE	PURPOSE OF TRAVEL	JOURNEY		ODOMETER READING			TOTAL MILES	
		From	To	Start	End	Distance (km)	Business	Private

Daily checks	Tires/ Wheel	Wipers	Lights	Mirrors	Horn	Seatbelts	Brakes	Coupling devices
Monday								
Tuesday								
Wednesday								
Thursday								
Friday								
Saturday								
Sunday								

Fuel Input				
Date	Quantity	Unit	Mileage	Units

Notes :

Signature :

Vehicle Mileage Logbook

Sheet no.:

Make :	Model :	Year :	License number :

DATE	PURPOSE OF TRAVEL	JOURNEY		ODOMETER READING			TOTAL MILES	
		From	To	Start	End	Distance (km)	Business	Private

Daily checks	Tires/ Wheel	Wipers	Lights	Mirrors	Horn	Seatbelts	Brakes	Coupling devices
Monday								
Tuesday								
Wednesday								
Thursday								
Friday								
Saturday								
Sunday								

Fuel Input				
Date	Quantity	Unit	Mileage	Units

Notes :

Signature :

Vehicle Mileage Logbook

Sheet no.:

Make :	Model :	Year :	License number :

DATE	PURPOSE OF TRAVEL	JOURNEY		ODOMETER READING			TOTAL MILES	
		From	To	Start	End	Distance (km)	Business	Private

Daily checks	Tires/ Wheel	Wipers	Lights	Mirrors	Horn	Seatbelts	Brakes	Coupling devices
Monday								
Tuesday								
Wednesday								
Thursday								
Friday								
Saturday								
Sunday								

Fuel Input				
Date	Quantity	Unit	Mileage	Units

Notes :

Signature :

Vehicle Mileage Logbook

Sheet no.:

Make :	Model :	Year :	License number :

DATE	PURPOSE OF TRAVEL	JOURNEY		ODOMETER READING			TOTAL MILES	
		From	To	Start	End	Distance (km)	Business	Private

Daily checks	Tires/ Wheel	Wipers	Lights	Mirrors	Horn	Seatbelts	Brakes	Coupling devices
Monday								
Tuesday								
Wednesday								
Thursday								
Friday								
Saturday								
Sunday								

Fuel Input				
Date	Quantity	Unit	Mileage	Units

Notes :

Signature :

Vehicle Mileage Logbook

Sheet no.:

Make : | Model : | Year : | License number :

DATE	PURPOSE OF TRAVEL	JOURNEY		ODOMETER READING			TOTAL MILES	
		From	To	Start	End	Distance (km)	Business	Private

Daily checks	Tires/ Wheel	Wipers	Lights	Mirrors	Horn	Seatbelts	Brakes	Coupling devices
Monday								
Tuesday								
Wednesday								
Thursday								
Friday								
Saturday								
Sunday								

Fuel Input				
Date	Quantity	Unit	Mileage	Units

Notes :

Signature :

Thank you!

WE ARE GLAD THAT YOU PURCHASED OUR BOOK!
PLEASE LET US KNOW HOW WE CAN IMPROVE IT!
YOUR FEEDBACK IS ESSENTIAL TO US.

Contact us at:

log'Sin@gmail.com

JUST TITLE THE EMAIL 'CREATIVE' AND WE WILL GIVE YOU SOME EXTRA SURPRISES!

CPSIA information can be obtained
at www.ICGtesting.com
Printed in the USA
LVHW052007051222
734629LV00013B/993

9 781803 851822